Home of the Blues:

Poems for the Spirit, Heart, and Soul

By: Joe Griffin, Ph.D.

In connection with Dr. Joe's Poetry and Writing Company, LLC

Copyright 2022

Written in connection with Dr. Joe's Poetry and Writing Company LLC c/o Dr. Jo-Seph (Joe) Griffin. All rights reserved. No part of this book may be reproduced, stored, copied in a retrieval system or transmitted in any form or by any means without proper written permission from the publishers, except by a retriever who may quote brief passages in a review to be printed in a newspaper, magazine, or journal.

First printing

Dr. Joe's Poetry and Writing Company LLC.
Dr. Jo-Seph Griffin
14744 Washington Avenue, #130
San Leandro, California 94578
Tel: (662) 313-6018 Email: joegriffin365@gmail.com
Website: drjoeswritingcompany.com

Photography Credits:

Delta Blues Museum
1 Blues Alley
Clarksdale, MS 38614

Free clip art from clipart-library.com

About the Author and Introduction

As I think about my life's journey from one of the poorest places in America, The Mississippi Delta, I am invigorated. Clarksdale, Mississippi, "The Home of the Blues,"(60 miles South of Memphis, Tennessee) placed a sense of urgency in me to share my written expression gift with anyone who will read or listen. I am thankful to have grown up there, as my experiences at home trained me to survive anywhere, anytime. My love and loyalty stem from the place I call home, although I currently live in and love Oakland, California and the Bay Area, where I serve as a poet, school administrator, and motivational speaker.

I stayed in trouble first through ninth grade, often being referred to the office twice in a period, until I became seriously involved in athletics in high school. I would make A's and B's, but D's and F's in conduct caused me to miss the honor roll. Through it all, my love for writing and my passion for basketball has always placed me in a peaceful mental state, and I long to never lose my love for either of those hobbies. I had no idea that I would be an undergraduate major in English with the ability to teach it at all levels, elementary through senior college, by the time I was done with school. I started writing poetry in sixth grade, and I plan to continue diving into the future with my words. This work ethic propelled me to obtain athletic and academic scholarships to a junior college HBCU and to a private, liberal arts undergraduate institution, to begin this journey after growing up in a Clarksdale neighborhood.

My professional experiences in education as a K-12 teacher, junior college and university English and Health professor, state-championship assistant coach and head coach, assistant principal, and principal have further equipped me to work well with others, as well as to be a motivator to all. I look for the best in all people, and these are the characteristics I hope to build in individuals versus exploiting one's weaknesses. We all make the world go around, and we can accomplish so much together through love and teamwork.

My experience with my family has taught me the importance of aspiring for more, whether the situation is good or bad. I believe in all humankind, and I even have faith in some people I don't know and have not met. Alternatively, school and education have played an integral role in my progression as a human, and it is through this lens I continue to aspire for betterment, growth, and continuous achievement. I would like to place other writers and aspiring writers in situations whereby they have the tools and resources to navigate the waters toward authorship. Therefore, I have established Dr. Joe's Poetry and Writing Company, LLC to help edit, revise, produce, present, and, ultimately, publish literary pieces.

This collection of poems, *Home of the Blues: Poems for the Spirit, Heart, and Soul,* is a continuum of moods. *The Blues* section explores the origin of the blues and the bluesy spirits of pain and deep thought. The *Love* section explores beautiful ideas about someone special or something loved or heartfelt. Finally, the *Motivation* section is fuel for the soul of individuals desiring to be better, do more, see further, or feel joy before, during, or after any struggle. We all aspire for greatness in some form. Connect with yourself, find yourself, and place yourself in each of the poems to allow total immersion within the walls of the following pages, my friends. There's a nugget in each work just for you.

Acknowledgments & Dedications

First of all, I must acknowledge the higher power which leads and guides me to create words with meaning. Without this power, there is no me, and my creativity does not exist.

Secondly, I have to acknowledge the roles that all the schools I have attended have played in pushing me forward in my quest for literary greatness. Those districts and schools are:

Clarksdale Municipal School District (K-12, HS Diploma), Clarksdale, Mississippi
Coahoma Community College (A. A. in English), Clarksdale, Mississippi
Belhaven University (College) (B. A. in English), Jackson, Mississippi
Delta State University (M.Ed. in Secondary Education), Cleveland, Mississippi
University of West Alabama (24 graduate hours in English), Livingston, Alabama,
The University of Southern Mississippi (Ed.S. and Ph.D.in Educational Leadership),
Hattiesburg, Mississippi (Dissertation Committee Members: Dr. Shelley, Dr. Lee, Dr. Benigno, Dr. Mohn, 2020)

This book is dedicated to my mother, who raised me as a single parent along with her mother, my grandmother. My mother's scholarship, as a student and as an English professor, along with the monetary bribes for me to read books as a youth, helped me decide to major in English when I was only interested in playing collegiate basketball.

This book is dedicated to my father because he stepped up his leadership and guidance during my adolescence at a time when I was headed in a different direction. As a result, I released much of the pain and bitterness from younger years after learning the difference and distance between men and women. My father is one of my most precious pairs of listening ears now. It's called healing.

This book is dedicated to my sons, Joezon (23) and Jayden (14). Just by their presence, those two young men have pushed me farther than they'll ever know. Seeing them progress into men keeps me hungry for life and living.

This book is dedicated to my sister, Venesia Griffin-Brown. Her strength through her most recent illness has made me even more proud to be her sibling. She is a fighter who will battle until the end. The half-eagle and half-lion (Griffin) in us arouses tenacity and strength.

This book is dedicated to all my other siblings, family members, and others who have encouraged me to share my poetry for countless years at family reunions and social events.

This book is dedicated to all aspiring writers that come before me and those that will come after me! We can do this y'all. Please enjoy *Home of the Blues: Poems for the Spirit, Heart, and Soul.*

Table of Contents

Blues (In My Spirit)

Home Of The Blues...2
The Blues Is, The Blues Are......................................4
For The Record..5
From Pain To Great..6
I Ponder Life Differently Now..................................7
Misunderstood...9
Time Elapses..10
What If?..12
Unbearable Hurt..13
Days Come Back..14
This Family I Know..15
I'm Hurting..16
Not Right..17

Love (In My Heart)

It's All About You..19
I Love, I Want..20
Joy...21
What Do Our Children Need?................................22
It Is You I Treasure..23
Last Night (I'll Never Forget It!)............................24
It's Super Real (The Way You Make Me Feel).........25
First Open Up..26
My Baby..27
My Worthy One..28
This Here Love Is True...29
I Love My Skin (The Skin I'm In)...........................31
For My Dear Lady..33

Motivation (For the Soul)

Rise, Grind, And Shine 35
I Aspire 37
Only Bright Days Remain 39
Be The B-E-S-T (Best) 40
A Guide 41
I Contemplate With No Doubt 42
Take Your Gift And Run 44
I Take It On Me 45
I Am Headed In A New Direction 47
Watching, Thinking, And Planning 49
Walls 50
What Drives The Man In Me? 51
Be True 53

Exiting Words 54

BLUES
(In My Spirit)

Home Of The Blues

Home of the Blues, where it all began
It's home to me…from Clarksdale, Mississippi, I am.
Where Robert Johnson sold his soul for guitar ability,
The blues are real here, one of America's most impoverished communities.

Home to Big Jack Johnson and Howlin Wolf
Home to Son House, John Lee Hooker, and my late, great-cousin, Mr. Sam Cooke
That's right, Coahoma County, we're on the map.
Home to Ike Turner, who played a part in many nationwide tracks.

Home to Earl Hooker and Eddie Boyd
Guitars, harmonicas, saxes, trombones, and all types of bluesy noise
Home to Willie Brown and Lil Green
The blues were born here, now forever on the scene.

Home to the one and only Muddy Waters
The blues are real here; remember Wesly Jefferson and Junior Parker,
And Princetop Perkins, my neighbor O.B. Buchana, my friend Bo Dolla, and others.
The Home of the Blues gave birth to music for many sisters and brothers.

And although he doesn't sing the blues, I can't forget "The Biggest Boss."
Clarksdale, Mississippi also bred the Iconic Rick Ross.
And it's even where Nate Dogg got his soulful singing start.
And now it's Grammy award-winning Kingfish's turn to run up the blues charts.

A worldwide brand is the "Down Home Blues."
These artists left and will leave many songs from which to choose.

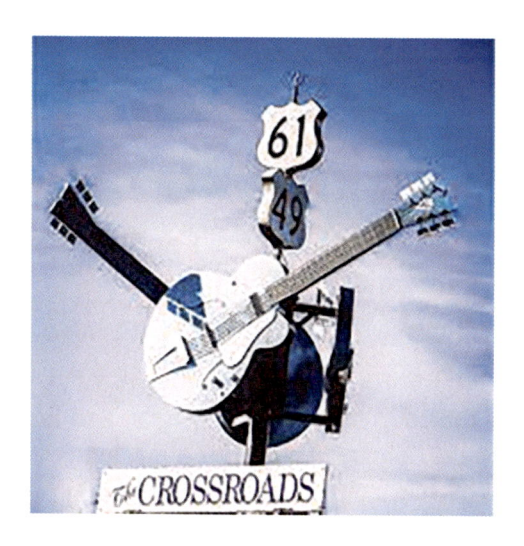

The Blues Is, The Blues Are

The blues *is* the everyday experience that bonds us all.
The joys and the pains of life, the good and the bad,
The highs and the lows, the ins and outs,
That tell a story or stories…the blues *are* an emotional, endless epic.

The blues *is* that painful relationship that brought about love.
Or that loving relationship that turned into terrible pain.
The blues *is* that feeling of exhilaration or the taste of trauma.
The blues *is* the confusion of those closest to you, maybe not understanding.

The blues *are* collages of feelings…
Feelings expressed in spirit but never said yet.
The blues *are* the loves of our lives.
The blues *are* our scars and our empowerments.

The blues *are* our roots for continuous growth.
Growth comes in many shapes, designs, and fashions.
The blues *is* the bounce in our steps on a cloudy afternoon.
The blues *is* what factors into our total being.

The blues *are* what we see and hear.
Yet, the blues *are* what we don't know about and never will.
The blues *are* the energies that teach us.
The blues *are* what makes the world go around.

The blues can be, but the blues *is* not just one thing.
The blues *are* a lot; it's our pain, love, and motivation.
The blues *is* or the blues *are* our rhythms to every sound.
The blues *are* what's keeping us afloat amidst it all.

For The Record

For the record, let it be stated…
This brother can't be replicated.
No, I can't be faded.
Coast to coast…move at will… and never mandated!
Let me go on by saying I'm rejuvenated.
Paid the price as a black man to get educated.
Came to Cali… Mississippi, for now, vacated.
All because I refuse to be regulated.
Alive and well, not sedated.
Change-maker that is truly dedicated.
Love for all is always demonstrated.
Vibe so strong, never been duplicated!
Always low-key and reserved… that's how I played it.
So savvy, not to be illustrated.
Full of life… no disrespect, but as if impregnated.
Happy as can be, ready to be elevated!
Ready for more, and I will not be placated…
But past experiences still have my heart security-gated.

From Pain To Great

I smile to push back the tears.
The pain burns as I think of the past years.
Many times I've been torn and remade.
My heart bleeds as if cut by a blade.

I laugh at the hurt and refuse to lose.
Barriers overcome, I have paid my dues.
Relishing the moment that I reach the top,
Anger subsides; eventually, it stops.

I embrace my flaws and will persist.
Blessed by the best, my heart is still bliss.
Knowing these pains will turnover dividends,
It forced me into motion, and now I'm setting trends.

I greet everything bad in me with all my good.
Positives outweigh the negatives, with love and strength understood.
Surviving the tough times, relying on rest to remain first-rate,
The hurt pushes me and fuels me from pain to great.

My pain will not stifle my motivation, as I am destined for greatness!

I Ponder Life Differently Now

I ponder life from a different perspective now.
Life is so deep, so real, and all about how.
As a minority, how do I battle the masses?
As a student, how do I put myself in a position to pass all my classes?

I ponder life differently now.
Life is a rollercoaster, a battle against the ocean, all about how.
As a leader, how do I lead when we are sometimes thought to be inferior?
As a dreamer, how can I gain the upper hand and become superior?

I ponder life quite differently now.
Life is full of emotions, opinions, and perspectives, and all about how.
As a black man, how do I make myself equal without showing anger?
As an optimist, how do I beat the odds, live past twenty-five, and avoid danger?

I ponder life from a drone view now.
Life's about one's vision, mission, and all about how.
As a citizen, how can I reach back to help someone else also feel success?
As a humanitarian, how can I spread love and knowledge, knowing I'm so blessed?

I ponder life differently these days.
Life is a journey, a training ground, and not all get to stay.
As one with ambition, how can I make my existence count?
As a parent, how can I ensure that to something my kids amount?

Yes indeed. I ponder life entirely differently from how I once did.
Life's a good, memory-filled teacher with ups and downs…
And through it, my path becomes more and more vivid.
I ponder life quite differently now.

Misunderstood

I sit down and appear emotionless,
Yet I am filled with emotions.
Words that I may speak
Or even my style of dress
Cannot partially display
The feelings I possess.
My face remains constant and blank,
Yet my heart is twisted
In many directions.
Soul-thoughts and ideas
Have been internally covered by paint
Because the energy released
Could cause me to faint.
Strong in body
As well as in mind,
Yet no one knows what I feel.
I know not myself at times,
And periods like these
Beg the stoic within to resign.
Staring nonchalantly into never-never space,
Yet I see no stars.
Suppressed intuitions have taken over the race,
Causing many of my gestures
Of the heart to be misplaced.
So misunderstood

Time Elapses

Time elapses so fast.
Too fast
So fast that I've been distant
When I've needed to be near.
I mean it hasn't slowed down one bit.
Although I appear to be bald,
My hair ruffles in the wind
As if full like the moon.
I just pray to live one more day.
Time spent here is just moving too swiftly.
With pain constantly invading my domain,
I don't know what to do next. . .
However, I apply, analyze, synthesize and evaluate.
To myself, burdens are heavy.
What's next? …
I think, but my thoughts run really rapidly repetitively.
To the world, sorrow enumerates endlessly.
Why?
War for oil, befriend a terrorist—
sloooow down.
This is happening all too quickly!
Too much data, too many facts, so many memories…
Time needs to pause briefly
So I can catch my breath.
Criminal activities of all kinds,
Home invasions, murder sprees, fraudulent conspiracies,

Technology heists, and other preyful plots…
What's a human to do?
Profile me, belittle me, don't count my vote.
Never raise me, show no love, for me have no hope.
Love's in my heart regardless.
For the end is here or near…
Time just elapses way too fast.

What If?

What if birds didn't have wings that allow them to fly?
What if the rain reaped a rinse that was boiling hot?
What if there was no criminal activity or violence?
What if the movie of life forewarned its plot?

What if the beautiful, brisk blue skies were green?
What if the orange, vibrant sun was blue?
What if there was no gravity assisting our existence?
What if there was no higher power guiding us and telling us what to do?

What if the tense, tidal oceans froze?
What if all the rugged California mountains collapsed?
What if money didn't spend and was no good?
What if no one could think and everyone snapped?

What if it was all likes and love, allowing us all just to get along?
What if respect, friendship, and hard work were all we knew?
What if there were no pain, pressure, or even death?
What if, what if these things were true?

Unbearable Hurt

It's an unbearable hurt that I must bear.
I opened my heart when I had closed it for years.
I had shut off my true, deep feelings,
Masked in meaningless relationships but never tears.

My divorce from my youngest son's mother,
Didn't put me anywhere close to where I now am.
Cash app after cash app, facetime after facetime,
And now you don't give a damn.

Out of nowhere, or is it because I, too, have struggles,
And was I really doing too much?
You first slowed down our convo;
Then you limited our physical touch.

Our vibe is very different now,
Yet, you still need help every week.
You also know how much I love you.
And you know how you make me weak.

You take from me and take from me,
Preying on my kindness.
Is love really real? Is this what I've missed?
Or is it that love covers you in blindness?

This hurt that I feel is quite unbearable;
Yet, it is this pain that I must bear.
Does true love exist for me? Is there one person for me?
And is there one person who'll return my same level of care?

Because this is an unbearable hurt that I'm bearing.

Days Come Back

The days of yesteryear are now behind me.
I constantly wish to bring them back.
I realize that they vanished and are gone for good,
But if I could re-track, my bags would be packed.

The days of pure happiness and bliss seem to be no more.
Joy sits in the backseat and has been replaced with Routine.
Bills, work, two sons that I love dearly, and other
Responsibilities have taken a step onto the scene.

Those carefree days that I enjoyed and used to know
Have evaporated into shrunken hours.
Firsthand experiences with racism and discrimination
Trouble me daily because I dream of obtaining powers.

Those good ol' days have passed but are not forgotten,
And contentment is on the way to save my life.
Love pervades my heart at all times.
I have no regrets because I try to live right.

Days come back in another form, please.

This Family I Know

There's a family that I know.
They don't eat a whole lot.
Shucks, they don't eat regularly.
The mother is strung out on heroin and crack.
The father got her hooked.
This is what their children see daily.
It is the only life that is real to them.
The oldest son, only 14, vows it won't be him.
He starts selling dope to his parents…
And paying the bills at the house…
Who's in charge now?
How can this young man do good
In a society in which he has only seen negativity?
Hope—there's not much of that.
So the twelve-year-old brother joins in, too.
They shelter their ten-year-old sister,
Showering her with gifts and money.
Her mind becomes infiltrated by material things.
And the only men she will entertain
Will be just like her brothers.
It's hard to make it out
When all you know is bad.
This family sank as so many have.

I'm Hurting

There are feelings buried within me that even
I have yet to see.
If it is at all possible to see a feeling.
Sometimes I think I'll explode because
Words often become trapped.
Repression is what the scholars call it.
I can be riding down the road and remember
An incident that was long forgotten.
I put it out of the way so I will not have to
Deal with it that day.
Even so, it still comes back to haunt me.
There have been several episodes like this.
I guess one can only forget for a moment.
I sometimes cry for the first time
About something old.
Pain is in my heart.
I'm hurting right now.
Although I live a lively life,
This hurt feels infinite.
Although it's my hope
That it's temporary.
I flash in and out of memories.
And it's ok if I bounce back and forth.
I'm surviving as best as I know how.
As my hurt will not bring me down any further.

Not Right

Understand the way of the world.
It is not fair, nor often is it right.
Jealousy, envy, hate, and despair rule.
Yet, there is hope…
Hope that one day things will improve.
Society needs betterment.
People need better judgment.
Betterment is the only way.
How can things get worse?
It is bad enough as it is.
The pressures of society are many;
The weak fold quickly.
I won't be the one to give in.
Deceit, misconceptions, and misinterpretations
Too often decide the outcomes of men and women.
It should not be like this.
This just ain't right!
War, bigotry, diseases of all kinds.
Covid one, two, three, and more.
Not to mention cancers that eat us up;
Where do these things come from?
High blood pressure, diabetes,
And so many unknown or rare illnesses
Then we talk about living.
Death prior to dishonor,
Is this still a livable creed?
Homelessness, suicide…homicides galore.
Snatch and grabs, follow and robs,
What happened to not hurting our neighbor?
This makes it tough for some to love themselves.
I'm a fan of life and living,
But not of this…this just ain't right.

LOVE
(In My Heart)

It's All About You

Walk like that!
Do what you do, girl.
I love it when you stroll by me.
Can I walk?
Can I talk?
Can I just be your friend?
Give a smart remark.
Be feisty—be you.
Something about you excites me.
What's your number?
Where do you live?
Can I come by just to speak?
Smile! It's alright.
Show some leg; you got it.
You're killing me softly with those eyes.
Can I take you out?
Will you come over?
Do you want to be mine?
It's all about you, girl.
It's all about you.

I Love, I Want

I love to hear your voice
And talk with you about forbidden things.
I want to be with you forever,
Sharing all our hopes and dreams.
I love to know that you are near—
To hold you and kiss you is real.
I want to be your husband,
Letting you have all of me and all I feel.
I love that you have ambition
Because a pair with goals is so great.
I want now to be next to you,
My heart won't allow me to wait.
I love when you touch me,
You make me feel so good.
I want you never to leave me,
And to keep you, I'll do what I should.
I love the way you look always,
Superior is one way to describe it.
I want you to know that I love you
Because I can't fight it or hide it!
I love the way you dress, your hair,
Your speech, your walk, and your intellect.
I want to be with you, there for you,
To have you, and I won't settle for less.
I love and want you every day!

Joy

Joy is when I see myself in either of my sons.
It's when an angel whispers advice in my ear.
I used to feel big joy when income tax rolled around.
When I've helped an elder, joy exudes.
Joy is advising the youth to have a dream.
It's the feeling of paying the month's bills.
I felt joy when my kids were five years old and spelled a word.
When I've worked hard to reach a goal, I feel joy.
Joy pervades when I see others joyful.
It's sitting back on a full stomach to watch t.v.
I feel joy when I think about my freedom.
When I'm complimented or encouraged, joy fills me up.
Joy is when I'm blessed to see a new year or a new day.
It's when I get that laugh that I've needed all week long.
I feel joy when loved ones are happy or proud of me.
When a friend makes good on a promise, joy arouses.
Joy is when I learn something I never knew.
It's seeing and believing in the prosperity of the future.
I feel joy at the thought of seeing heaven.
When I realize life is still in me, my joy is strengthened evermore.

What Do Our Children Need?

What do our children need?
It's a deep and complex question.
They need confidence instilled in them.
They need support from their family.
They need encouragement.
They need love.
They need someone to believe in them.
They need someone to care for them.
Someone to stand by them…
Someone to lead and guide them…
They need so much.
Hope is needed.
Determination is needed.
A will to succeed is needed.
Hard work is needed.
Loyalty is needed.
They need people to take out time with them.
They need to be taught.
They need to be read to.
They need all these things and much, much more.
But they will only have what they see.
Because it's all they know.

It Is You I Treasure

My life, my love, my friend…
It is you that I'll be with until the end.
I need you and want you in all ways, always.
With you, I'll spend the rest of my days.
Your potential, your fight, your will,
It is these traits about you that bring me thrills.
Your walk, your talk, your smile,
For your love, I'd travel many, many miles.
Your eyes, your hair, your curves…
These are more traits about you
That bring uneasiness to my nerves.
Priceless, you are, and so is our love.
I'm so glad that you were sent to me from above.
I will not and cannot ever, ever let you go.
I love you with all my heart…
I want you to know.
Every day is an honor, and every day is a pleasure.
You are my love and my life…
It is you I treasure.
Thank you, my love.

Last Night (I'll Never Forget It!)

Last night was an experience of a lifetime;
I will never forget it, but I'll frequently relive it.
The actions were not planned in any way.
In fact, I think we tried to avoid it.
Even so, last night is now a fact,
And an act that I thoroughly enjoyed.
Never could I have imagined an atmosphere of the sort.
After all, you and I were the only two present.
Our eyes met at midnight, and there was no denying it.
I took you into my arms without refusal,
And the whole situation began to unfold.
I kissed you. You kissed me back.
After that, I simply laid back.
Soft seduction invaded us both,
Permeating the entire place for hours to follow.
To realize that we had so much energy built up
Within us tells me that tension had to be released.
Reproduction of last night's activities must occur soon.
No doubt, it must have been right.
Let's make more memories, but I'll never forget last night.

It's Super Real
(The Way You Make Me Feel)

The way you make me feel!
Oh my god, it's super real.
You make my heart freeze… like still.
Make my soul feel light.
Oh my god, you make my feelings take flight.
What can I do to calm myself?
Better yet, what can I do without you?
Being with you makes me more, indeed not less.
Oh this feeling is so true.
Step up to the plate as my date.
Kings need queens– I mean to say they deserve.
Queens need kings to help them calm their nerves.
Take my hand, and let's leave them all where they stand.
I'm the man, and I've got our plan.
I'm having fun right now, but I'm not playing.
The way you make me feel,
Oh my god, it's super real.

First Open Up

Why deny the feeling?
Especially when that feeling feels good…
First, open up, let your hair down,
Understand what to do and do it like you should.

Don't put your feelings down!
Especially when these feelings really bring you up…
Relax, relate, release,
Let nature take its course; listen to your gut.

Share your feelings openly,
Just as light shines.
Listen, be yourself, cute, intelligent,
Afterwhile you could very well be mine.

Let me feel that you feel that I am your man.
Similar to a quarterback or point guard,
I will lead, assist, and help you;
Lovers need each other because times get hard.

Your feelings will reflect my feelings,
So don't hold back and treat me right.
I see endless potential and possibilities with you,
And one day we might be together every night.

But first, open up.

My Baby

My baby, my baby
She's just misunderstood.
Intelligent, sweet like water,
Makes me feel so good!

My baby, my baby
A fireball of passion and love
Smart, sexy, hot like fire,
And I can't help but touch.

My baby, my baby
Yes, she fusses, but she can't help it.
She's just mad because I'm not always there,
But Mr. Goodbar comes around and settles it.

My baby, my baby
So caring when zaddy's around
When I'm not, she's quitting me and cussing me.
Til daddy comes back to town.

My baby, my baby
Knows that neither of us will leave
Love so strong and feels so good,
I know it's sometimes hard to believe.

But believe this…you are my baby!

My Worthy One

This poem or story is about my worthy girl.
She could be you or your guy or girl in your mind.
However, she's pretty, sexy, and silky like wine.
I have to have her in my world.

She's here, y'all; she finally made it.
Home with me, where she should be,
Grasping, touching, and holding me tightly.
Time felt still, but patiently I waited.

So good to see you, even better to touch.
Sensual, smooth, gentle, sincere,
Intelligent, ambitious, supreme, pure,
This kind of love is more than mere lust.

So badly I wish to experience this love.
Dreaming of our time together,
Planning a plan to make it last forever,
For my girl is worthy of my trust.

This Here Love Is True

Oh my God, oh my God
Yes indeed!
The way you make me feel,
I feel like a fiend in sooo much need.

When I'm missing you,
I just don't know what to do.
Oh my god, oh my god
Will you come with me?

Why'd you leave me?
Why'd you put us on hold?
Why'd you tell me you got stuff going on?
When it's you I want to hold.

At night, when the lights are off,
It's you that I think of.
It's you for which I have so much…
Shhh, be quiet… I'm saying love.

Yes, it's early.
It's only been a matter of weeks.
But this feeling I get down in my knees,
When I think of you, it makes my heart weak.

Why'd you take our love away?
Why won't you just dive in?
I understand that you're fresh out of a relationship;
I know you're trying to mend.

But it would feel good
Knowing that you do care.
Tell me every once in a while.
For you, I'm going to be there.

Ask me for what you need.
If I got it, you got it too.
That's what it is, baby!
This here love is true.

I Love My Skin (The Skin I'm In)

I love my skin, the skin I'm in
Loving the skin I'm in
You should love yours, too.
We all make the world go round and round.
I love the diversity of melanin.
My skin comes in shades that are smooth.
My skin comes in shades that are rich.
My skin comes in shades that appear pure.
Oh, so deep and complex is the skin I'm in.

Loving the skin I'm in
You should love yours, too.
Different people possess different dynamics.
I love the circumstances surrounding my being.
My skin represents strength.
My skin tells so many stories.
My skin, however, is of a chosen destiny.
Oh, so humble and unrelenting is the skin I'm in.

Loving the skin I'm in
I hope you love yours, too.
We're not the same but of the same.
I love our simple coexistence.
My skin is the light at the end of the journey.
My skin is hope and love rebirthed.
My skin does not crack along with my heart.

Oh, so triumphant and resilient is the skin I'm in.

For My Dear Lady

Intellect flows from you like a river.
Sunshine is what you provide.
You are the moon because you keep me high;
Nature calls for us to be together.

Beautiful you are in all ways.
Your sexiness cannot be denied.
Your smile sheds light,
And your femininity is very true.

I can talk to you because you listen.
In return, I love listening to you.
The things you say often make me think;
You are indeed a good influence.

I crave your body from head to all toes.
The energy we release when together is no lie.
I want to be near you, with you, under you,
Around you, behind, and beside you at all times.

MOTIVATION
(For the Soul)

Rise, Grind, And Shine

This creed is official!
And I'm ready to do my part.
I'm ready to make my pledge.
I'm ready for my start.
Rise, grind, and shine, I must!

Yes, I'm focused.
I'm sure about what I want.
Nothing can stop this movement;
I'm putting in the work; blessings will come.
Rise, grind, and shine, I will!

I'm finally finished with school.
Obstacles must be faced.
I come from the hood where I saw things:
Poverty, gang wars, violence, not to mention my race.
Rise, grind, and shine, I shall!

Tomorrow is not promised.
This I should surely know.
But today awaits me.
There's no limit to how far I can go.
Rise, grind, and shine. I want it!

Getting rest every night,
But not oversleeping plans or work
Believing in the dream,
Knowing before success often comes hurt
Rise, grind, and shine. I won't stop!

Told that I wouldn't make it
My, oh, my, today that fuels my fire.
Each day I wake with hope and a work ethic
To have what the heart desireth.
Rise, grind, and shine… I have no choice!

I Aspire

I aspire,
First of all, to believe.
Belief is fundamental
To play on "Team Succeed."
I aspire to better myself daily,
To positively influence others,
And to keep a good attitude
With all my earthly sisters and brothers.
I aspire to be the person
That many people can't,
To be humble and self-reliant,
Feet solidly planted.
I aspire to uplift humanity in some form,
To remain optimistic
Well beyond the norm.
I aspire to stand up for right
Even if deemed wrong,
To be a soldier of honor,
Though the hours seem long.
I aspire to use every little gift
That has been given to me,

To be the master of my faith,
Writer of my destiny.
I aspire to set a good example
For those I lead,
To push and grow through the Earth,
Like a well-rooted seed.

Only Bright Days Remain

The sun will shine regardless.
Even if it rains, the sun will shine.

Only bright days remain—
That's the motto that pushes me.
I understand that no one animal will stop a show.
When things go wrong, they still will get better.

Only bright days remain—
I know this is true, and I can't quit now.
Broken down, broke, sick, misunderstood,
I still must survive and push forward.

Only bright days remain—
I have had many storms, and I am covered.
My hunger overrules my thirst;
I know I can operate in a way to feel successful.

Only bright days remain—
I have been wronged from many angles,
And I still see the worst for their best.
I believe love overpowers the pain I know.

Only bright days remain—
Nothing earthly can hold me back.
Until I die or unless I'm dead,
No matter the struggle, positiveness is ahead.

Only bright days remain—
I'm a fighter that will fight until the very end!

Be The B-E-S-T (Best)

I put my heart into everything I do…
It's all I've ever done…
All the greats have done it,
Whether Gretzky, Jordan, Step, or Lebron.

This is all I know,
How to be the B-E-S-T- best
How to get and stay on top
How to struggle through tough times, passing any and all tests

Conquer all, and be the most…
Settle…. Never!
We can't do that because a lot is riding on this…
We must always remain clever.

Whatever the situation, whatever is going on,
My life, your life, or hers or his,
We must do what's right because we know right.
We are here, and it's the good life we wish to live.

A Guide

Remember the best times; block out the bad.
Try to stay happy; no one wishes to be sad.
Love life, living, and all that goes along.
Do what is right, and avoid wrong.

Know your surroundings; always be aware.
Stand up, be strong, and make an effort to be fair.
Keep your eyes on the prize; reach for your goals.
Listen to your supporters, and leave the doubters out cold.

Never be satisfied; we deserve the best.
Even though it's a struggle, don't settle for less.
Know yourself; self-discipline is key.
There is no limit to what you can be.

This is a guide, don't stray away.
Promise to become better each and every day.
Live your life; don't forget to have fun.
Love God, others, and yourself; you'll get things done.

I Contemplate With No Doubt

I contemplate on the last few years.
Joy, pain, and reminiscing bring me to tears.
My heart shines through all I do.
Encountered issues, stayed focused, stayed true…
A demon, a villain,
Attempted to bring me down.
Whether it's the boss, an ex, or a hater–
I refuse to go down.
Jealousy permeates…
Why? I do not care to know
I do know, however, no one
Can stop my ability to grow.
Race ahead to the number one spot–
I am what I am.
Belittle me, can't stop me—
About your ill feelings, I don't give a damn.
I'm an animal–
A hungry, hungry beast.
Motivation is what it is to me–
A soldier, at least.
Throw slang, curse me,
Attempt to defame
And slander my name.
I was born to be tough–
Refuse to fall weak or lame.

Situations have molded me,
Made me strong.
Prepared now for life in all ways–
You can't tell me I don't belong.
Refusing to bow down but ready
For what I see and can't see.
Reality has settled in,
And I'll never doubt what I can be.

Therefore, I contemplate with no doubt.

Take Your Gift And Run

Take your gift and run, son!
Take your gift and run like the sun.
If not, your gift will not blossom as it should.

Take your gift, and be a star.
Take your gift, and bless us with it by far.
Don't be selfish with your gift.

Take your gift, and fear not.
Take your gift, and be a bright spot.
Your gift is your opportunity.

Take your gift, and shine bright.
Take your gift, and shine so right.
Your gift defines and deserves you.

Take your gift, and do not lose.
Take your gift because life's for you to choose.
Your gift can take you where many minds allude.

Whatever you do…Please…
Just take your gift and run, son.
Take your gift and run like the sun.

I Take It On Me

I take it on me to be me.
I take it on you to be you.
Whatever you do,
However you feel;
Your will must be right
For dreams to be fulfilled.
Dream.
Live.
See…
Have.
Share.
Be…
Designate a place for your living.
There's no receiving,
If there's no actual giving.
Comprehend.
Know.
Want.
Thirst.
Hunger… Go get it!
The situation's already the worst.
Know when,
Know why.
Now you know right.
Business as usual,
Pleasure's out of sight.

Men be men,
Ladies, if you wish, be feminine.
All stand up,
And make differences or dividends.
Listen to help;
It's good for direction.
Meet deadlines and requirements
While always counting blessings.

I Am Headed In A New Direction

I am headed in a new direction…
Somewhere else, some other place.
I am sick and tired of being sick and tired.
Therefore, I have decided to change my course.

Nobody ever said I had to be satisfied.
I hate my predicament, so I am going somewhere.
Where am I going?
I don't know just yet, but I am leaving.

I am in search of happiness.
Happiness is not where I am right now.
Therefore, I've decided to pursue my dream.
My dream is the reason I'm leaving.

I am headed in a new direction.
Plans may go awry, but at least I must try.
I will leave here tonight because things aren't right.
My dreams and goals will not take a backseat to your thoughts and beliefs.

I am headed in a new direction.
I will take a new path to see different things.
I will succeed because failure has never, ever been an option.
I am headed in a new direction because I am a new person.

Watching, Thinking, And Planning

I watch any and all things,
Observing what happens daily;
Noting the mistakes of others
So that I may not succumb.

I think all the time.
I want to find a way out.
It is important and imperative
That the thought process does not decrease.

I'm planning when I speak;
Or even when the speaker speaks.
I plan while I bathe or exercise;
I will mastermind and execute my plans.

I'm watching, thinking, and planning,
Every minute of my existence.
I'm literally watching what I think,
So that I can execute my planning.

I watch everything within sight.
I think constantly about my situation.
I plan daily to perfect my dreams.
Watching, thinking, and planning leads to the real.

Walls

These walls are closing in on me.
My space becomes minimal.
Fear is not and will never, ever, be an option.
I muster the strength to save myself.
I will not be entrapped;
I will not become enslaved.
I refuse to give in or up.
Power overcomes pain and panic–
I rise hungrier than ever before.
Delusional? I say not!
These walls are about to collapse.
I spread my arms to protect my space.
This building is mine and only mine.
These circumstances, too, will soon pass me by.
I will endure until the very end.
I will not, at all,
Be misguided.
And I refuse to allow myself
To be misled.
Desire and determination overcome defeat.
I am now thirsty
As I've ever been.
Undeniable–
I know and feel so.
Walls, I need more than six feet.

What Drives The Man In Me?

Wow, what a question it is!
So many driving forces are behind the man in me.
From God to my sons to my ambitious soul
From my ancestors' struggles to my very own goals

Wow, what a question it is!
So many things have made the man in me.
From mistake to mistake to encounters with hate
From both grandmothers' deaths to early dealings with real estate

Wow, what a question it is!
So many experiences have shaped the man in me.
From hood standoffs to being cut from the basketball team
To captaining every team and living my hoop dream

Wow, what a question it is!
So many people have helped build the man in me.
From mom's sweetness to dad's harsh but eventual, real care
From Grandma's ruggedness to my family always being there

Wow, what a question it is!
So many emotions fill the man in me.
From *The Joys and Pains of Life* to feelings of power
From love to anger to strength; fortunately, never been a coward

Wow, what a question it is!
So many driving forces are behind my reality.
From where I've been to where I've come
To where I'll eventually be…these things drive the man in me.

Just know this man is driven!

Be True

Believe, struggle, work hard,
And there's no limit to what you can do.
Aim for the stars because they're not far,
To yourself be true.

Understand that there are ups,
But with ups also come downs.
Be committed to excellent achievement,
And great rewards and benefits will be found.

Realize that nothing comes easy;
If it does, it's probably not real.
Be hungry for what life has to offer,
And approach life with much zeal.

Push forward when times get tough,
And persist with a desire not to be denied.
Failure's not an option and means nothing…
If you truly, truly tried.

Be honest and true in all that you do,
And have faith that He will take care of you.

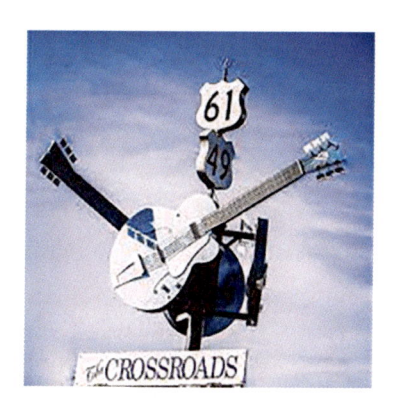

Exiting Words

Thank you for experiencing *Home of the Blues: Poems for the Spirit, Heart, and Soul* with me. Poetry comes naturally to me, but organizing those poems for a book is tricky despite all the scholarly work I've been blessed to complete. As a person who has been writing poetry since the sixth grade, my biggest fear is not getting the work out to the masses. This collection of poetry is the mere beginning of my efforts to influence everyone I come in contact with to live a happy, *bluesful* life. I also encourage everyone to keep love centered in our thoughts and actions, while keeping our souls rejuvenated and motivated to conquer obstacles that so often hold us back for one reason or another.

This book was written from coast to coast, literally, over many years. *The Joys and Pains of Life (2009)* preceded this work and is now out of print. I began to prepare to publish *Home of the Blues: Poems for the Spirit, Heart, and Soul* after completing and publishing my doctoral studies and dissertation at the University of Southern Mississippi, just before the pandemic in 2020. After experiencing personal trauma a year later, I relocated to California, where I have continued to prepare for publication over the past calendar year. I miss being able to just drop into my hometown, Clarksdale, Mississippi, but the Bay Area is opening up more visionary ideas that have recharged resiliency in me. I pledge to bring light and to be a light for others.

As a traditional poet, there is then the complex decision of whether your poems should rhyme or when they should rhyme. However, a poet has to go with the poems' arrangements that fit into the concept for that particular project. There are a variety of rhyming and non-rhyming poems in this collection and a variety of both styles in my catalog of work. The bluesful energy reflected within *Home of the Blues: Poems for the Spirit, Heart, and Soul* illustrates the blues as a lifestyle residing in our daily spirits, love as a powerful force within our hearts, and motivation as a vehicle for our souls.

As a 20-year veteran educator, including 14 years as principal, I have to show love to every student, teacher, parent, or community stakeholder that I encountered during my time as a turnaround principal. I have had opportunities to serve school communities in every region of Mississippi, in Louisiana, and now in Oakland, California. I love how each opportunity has molded me into what I am today. The options are few where I come from, and people sometimes need to be reminded that there's an area in the United States that is poorer than what you think is the poorest…a place that has fewer jobs than where you think there are only a few. I could go on and on, but that is also what gives us the hope that brighter days are ahead and attainable. I hope to inspire dreamfulness and hopefulness, unapologetically.

Look forward to varying collections and series of poems focused on youth leadership, equality, education, love for writing, faith, and other topics that I will begin organizing for print. I have established Dr. Joe's Poetry and Writing Company LLC to put myself and others in a position to go after literary aspirations, including editing, writing, speaking, publishing, etc. The opportunity is now, and in this new day and age, one's writing could be that thing that saves someone's spirit, that protects one's heart, and that inspires one's soul. Allow me to enter your realm.

Love,

Jo-Seph (Joe) Griffin AKA Joe Griffin AKA Dr. Joe AKA Gino AKA Joegino AKA Joe Jeezy
joegriffin365@gmail.com   drjoeswritingcompany.com

Made in the USA
Columbia, SC
21 June 2022